nor

CW00956947

favourites

by Lee Geok Boi

Fusion before the phrase was even coined, Nonya cuisine
represents a delightful blend of Chinese, Malay and other
Southeast Asian flavours and cooking styles.
Prepare all-time Nonya Classics such as Ayam Buah Keluak,
Duck Soup, Babi Pong Teh and Prawn Sambal with Petai.
The clear instructions and step-by-step photographs in
Nonya Favourites ensure delicious results every time.

PERIPLUS

The Nonya Kitchen

'Fusion' before the phrase was even coined, Nonya dishes successfully marry Southeast Asian herbs and spices with Chinese ingredients in a cuisine that is the culinary legacy of the Straits Chinese communities of Malaysia, Singapore and Indonesia.

The Straits, or Peranakan, Chinese trace their roots to the 15th century when predominantly male Chinese migrant traders settled in Southeast Asia and married local women. The male offspring of these unions were often repatriated to China for an education before returning to their newly adopted lands. The daughters, on the other hand, remained and were raised by their mothers before being married off within the community to forge important ties between families. In time, a distinct sub-ethnic group evolved with its own language, dress and, of course, kitchen. The men folk became known as 'Baba' and the women 'Nonya', the female term also lending itself to the glorious cuisine that ensued.

Nonya cuisine reflects the cultural mix of the community: from Malay cuisine were adopted ingredients such as *belacan*, chillies, lemongrass, galangal and turmeric, and, from Chinese cuisine, a fondness for pork and the requisite styles of food preparation. Later still, more ingredients were incorporated into the cuisine from Indian, Thai and Portuguese Eurasian kitchens.

In the past, there was enough wealth and leisure within the community for the women to devote their time to culinary arts and the preparation of elaborate meals. Although the richer Straits Chinese households employed domestic help, which made the grinding of spices, squeezing of coconut milk and pounding of *belacan* relatively easy, Nonyas of all social classes were not above enjoying a good gossip in the kitchen while preparing the basic ingredients essential to their cuisine.

Today, the food blender replaces the pestle and mortar and grinding stone in many Nonya households. The only exception to this is in the preparation of Sambal Belacan, a highly aromatic condiment that transforms simple fried fish or plain vegetables into something tantalizing—the heady aromas and earthy flavours of freshly pounded Sambal Belacan cannot be recreated by simple blending.

The curries, sambals, soups and braised pork dishes keep well and often have to be left to stand for an hour or so after cooking to allow the flavours to develop. Except in the one-dish noodle meals such as Mee Siam or Laksa, Nonya food is usually served with plain rice and eaten communally as with Chinese food. However, with the exception of soup, which is served individually with a soup spoon, Chinese-style, the traditional way to eat Nonya curries and sambals is Malay-style, by hand.

How to reduce preparation times

Although packaged spice pastes have given busy households an approximation of traditional Nonya food, these ready-to-use spice concoctions cannot compare to freshly prepared, homemade spice pastes. To make Nonya food a quick and easy affair, simply prepare a big batch of spice pastes and keep them frozen in ready-to-cook batches—even ground dried red chillies freeze well. Just don't forget to label the boxes clearly to prevent confusion later on.

How to thicken curries

To thicken and enrich a curry or sambal without adding to the spiciness, candlenuts are often added. A good substitute is macadamia nuts or raw almonds.

Glossary

Asam Gelugor: The dried slices of the sour fruit, *garcinia atnoviridis*, are sometimes used in place of tamarind pulp in Nonya dishes. If *asam gelugur* is not available, substitute with tamarind pulp.

Belacan: Shrimp paste is a quintessential ingredient in Nonya and Malay food. It comes in blocks and can vary from soft to firm and be a lurid pink or a dark gray-brown colour. It is now also available bottled in powder form. Although used in small amounts, the quality of the *belacan* affects the final flavour of the dish. Many Nonyas will swear by Penang *belacan* which is also my personal preference. If you are uncertain of the quality of your *belacan*, for example, if you think it smells rather strong, use less rather than more. Not enough is better than too much to prevent an imbalance in the flavours of your spice paste. The traditional way to measure *belacan* was by slices, but the best way to get a uniform measure is by spoonfuls. To measure, press some *belacan* into the measuring spoon and level off with a knife.

Cai Xin: A cousin of Chinese kale, *cai xin*, or *choi sum* as it is often known as, is one of the most versatile of Chinese greens. The easier it is to pierce the base of the stem with a fingernail, the more tender the vegetable.

Candlenuts: A round, cream-coloured waxy nut, often known by its Malay name, *buah keras*. Candlenuts are added to Nonya dishes for both flavour and texture, as they help to thicken a sauce.

Coconut Milk: Coconut milk is another essential Nonya ingredient. Fresh is best but UHT coconut milk works well for practically all Nonya dishes where the coconut milk has to be cooked. The coconut cream used in these recipes is UHT coconut cream which is very thick. Too much coconut milk in a curry or sambal makes a dish too rich besides being a cholesterol nightmare. However, too little will not bring out the flavours properly. The richness can be varied to suit personal tastes.

Fermented Soya Beans: known as *dou jiang* and usually sold in jars with the soft fermented and salted soya beans doused in a brownish liquid. The beans are usually mashed before using.

Galangal: Often measured by the thumb but it can also be measured by slices. Naturally, the measure can vary depending on the size of the root. However, it is not all that critical to get the quantity spot on.

Kale: Known by its Chinese name, *kai lan*, or baby *kai lan* for the smaller, rounder version. Kale has a robust flavour and texture and is slightly bitter. Although the lowest, hardest part of the stem may be discarded, the remainder should be cooked and enjoyed for its mild, crisp pith.

Lemongrass: Usually measured by the stalks. However, lemongrass is rarely uniform in size and some stalks can be rather small. Cup measures are therefore given to ensure a constant measure. Only the white bulbuous part of the stalk is used—this is the most fragrant part—the greenish upper part of the stalk is discarded. Trim away the woody root and peel away any dried-up outer layers. Slice thinly first to make blending easier.

Screwpine Leaves: Pandan leaves impart a subtle flavour to many Nonya dishes, both savoury and sweet. The leaves are either tied and left in the pot for savoury dishes, or pounded to extract the green colouring for desserts.

Tamarind: Dried tamarind fruits are often available in the form of a pulp which must be soaked in water, stirred, squeezed and strained to yield a sour yet flavoursome liquid. All forms of solids and remaining pulp should be discarded.

Condiments

Acar Nenas (Spicy Pineapple Pickle)

500 g (1 lb 2 oz) fresh
  pineapple, peeled
2 tablespoons oil
6 cm (2 ¹/2 in) ginger,
  peeled and sliced
1 medium fresh red chilli,
  deseeded and coarsely
  sliced
¹/2 teaspoon salt
2–3 drops dark soy sauce

3 tablespoons sugar
1 tablespoon vinegar

 Serves 4

Preparation time:
  20 mins
Cooking time:
  10 mins

1. Halve pineapple lengthways, then cut each half into
3 or 4 wedges. Remove hard core and cut each wedge
into 1 cm (¹/2 in) slices.
2. Heat oil in wok and sauté ginger slices and chilli for
about 2 minutes until fragrant.
3. Add pineapple, salt, dark soy sauce, sugar and vinegar and sauté, stirring constantly, for about 10 minutes
or until the oil rises to the surface and the pineapple
looks glossy. The pineapple should still be juicy.
4. Serve with plain rice and any coconut-based dish, or
with fried fish.

Acar Timun (Spicy Cucumber Pickle)

300 g (11 oz) cucumber
1 teaspoon salt for cucumber
100 g (3 ¹/2 oz) carrots
2 tablespoons oil
4 slices ginger
¹/2 teaspoon mustard seeds

1 teaspoon turmeric
  powder
¹/2 teaspoon chilli powder
¹/2 teaspoon sugar
¹/4 teaspoon salt
2 tablespoons rice vinegar

1. Halve cucumbers lengthwise and remove soft core.
Cut into 3 ¹/2 cm (1 ¹/2 in) juliennes.
2. Mix 1 teaspoon salt into cucumbers, set aside for
15 minutes then squeeze to extract as much juice as
possible.
3. Cut carrot into 3 ¹/2 cm (1 ¹/2 in) juliennes.
4. Heat oil in wok and sauté ginger and mustard seeds
until mustard seeds pop. Stir in turmeric and chilli powder, then add the cucumbers, carrot, sugar and salt and
sauté for a further 2 minutes. Take care not to overcook.
Turn off heat, add vinegar and mix well.
5. Cool in wok, then bottle the pickle. Serve only after
pickling overnight.

 Serves 4

Preparation time:
  20 mins
Cooking time:
  15 mins

Sambal Belacan (Fragrant Shrimp Paste Sambal)

25 medium fresh red
  chillies, deseeded
1 tablespoon shrimp paste
  (*belacan*), toasted

 Serves 4

Preparation time:
  20 mins
Cooking time:
  15 mins

1. Toast *belacan* on the back of a spoon over a naked flame, or dry-fry in a pan, or bake in foil until fragrant.
2. Pound chillies with toasted *belacan* until fairly smooth and store in a bottle in the fridge.

Note: *To prepare Sambal Belacan with Lime, stir 1 table-spoon lime juice into the finished Sambal Belacan and mix well or serve with sliced kalamansi limes.*

Nonya Mee
(Nonya Noodles)

4 tablespoons oil
25 g (¹/4 cup) shallots, sliced thinly
3 cloves garlic, chopped
1 tablespoon fermented soya beans (*dou jiang*), mashed well
300 g (11 oz) shelled small prawns
200 g (7 oz) mustard greens (*cai xin*), cut into finger-lengths
200 g (1 ¹/2 cups) beansprouts, rinsed and cleaned
800 g (1 lb 12 oz) cooked yellow noodles, rinsed
250 ml (1 cup) pork stock
¹/2 teaspoon salt

 Serves 4

Preparation time:
 15 mins
Cooking time:
 10 mins

1. Heat the oil in a wok and sauté the shallots until golden brown. Remove and set aside.
2. Add the chopped garlic and mashed soya beans to the wok and sauté until fragrant.
3. Add the prawns, vegetables and beansprouts. Sauté lightly and when the prawns are nearly cooked, add the salt, noodles and stock, and mix well.
4. Bring to the boil and cook for 2 minutes, stirring constantly. Finally, stir in the fried shallots. If desired, reserve some fried shallots as a garnish.
5. Serve at once with Sambal Belacan with Lime
(see recipe, page 5)

Mee Siam (Spicy Tangy Noodles)

Noodles

400 g (14 $^1/_2$ oz) dried rice
   noodles (*mifen*)
$^1/_2$ tablespoon ground
   dried red chillies
25 g ($^1/_4$ cup) shallots
1 tablespoon fermented
   soya beans (*dou jiang*)
2 tablespoons water
5 tablespoons oil
$^1/_2$ teaspoon salt
400 g (14 $^1/_2$ oz)
   beansprouts, rinsed
4 tablespoons water
2 tablespoons coconut cream

1. Soak the noodles in
water until soft but firm,
then drain and dry.
2. Grind together the
chillies, shallots, soya
beans and water until
smooth.
3. Heat the oil in a wok
and sauté the ground
ingredients with salt until
the oil rises to the surface.
4. Stir in the beansprouts,
then add the noodles,
water and coconut milk
and stir-fry for about 10
minutes or until the
noodles are cooked but
still al dente. If the mixture begins to burn,
sprinkle 1 tablespoon of
water and continue frying
until the noodles are
done. Leave the noodles
uncovered to cool until
the gravy and garnishing
items are ready.

Gravy

6 tablespoons oil
1 $^1/_4$ litres (5 cups) chicken
   stock or water
1 $^1/_2$ teaspoons salt
1 tablespoon tamarind
   pulp soaked in 250 ml
   (1 cup) water, stirred and
   strained
125 ml ($^1/_2$ cup) coconut
   cream
$^1/_2$ teaspoon sugar

Spice Paste

2 tablespoons fermented
   soya beans (*dou jiang*)
150 g (1 $^1/_2$ cups) shallots
1 tablespoon shrimp paste
   (*belacan*)
4 candlenuts (*buah keras*)
1 $^1/_2$ tablespoons ground
   dried red chillies

1. Grind or blend all the
Spice Paste ingredients
until smooth.
2. Heat the oil in a large
saucepan and sauté the
Spice Paste until fragrant
and the oil rises to the
surface.
3. Add the stock or water,
the strained tamarind
water and salt and bring
to the boil. Add the
coconut cream and sugar
and heat through but
avoid boiling to prevent
cream from separating.

Garnish

200 g (7 oz) firm beancurd,
   halved across
6 tablespoons oil
200 g (7 oz) small prawns
   with shells intact
$^1/_2$ teaspoon turmeric powder
2 eggs, hard-boiled, shelled
   and quartered
$^1/_2$ cup chopped chives
Chilli Oil (see recipe on
   opposite page)
6 limes, halved

1. To prepare the bean-
curd, heat the oil in a
wok and brown the
beancurd. Cool and slice
into strips.
2. To prepare the prawns,
rinse clean, then season
with $^1/_2$ teaspoon
turmeric. Fry the prawns
in the oil until brown. If
the prawns are very small,
the shells will turn crisp. If
the prawns are on the
large side, they will
become chewy.

To serve

1. Place some fried noo-
dles into a bowl. Ladle
hot gravy over the
noodles.
2. Garnish with egg,
beancurd, prawns, chives,
a dash of Chilli Oil and
half a lime.

Chilli Oil

1 teaspoon tamarind soaked
  in 2 tablespoons water
1 tablespoon ground dried
  red chillies
50 g (¹/2 cup) onion
2 tablespoons water
¹/4 teaspoon salt
¹/2 teaspoon sugar
3 tablespoons oil

1. Stir and strain the tamarind, discard solids.
2. Grind the chillies, onion and water until smooth.
3. Heat the oil in a small saucepan and sauté the ground chilli paste with salt and sugar until the oil rises to the surface. Add the tamarind water and continue cooking until the oil rises again.
4. Serve with Mee Siam.

 Serves 4

Preparation time:
  1 hour
Cooking time:
  30 mins

Laksa Lemak (Rice Noodle in Coconut Gravy)

2 tablespoons oil
1 litre (4 cups) prawn or
   chicken stock
250 ml (1 cup) thick
   coconut milk
800 g (1 lb 13 oz) fresh thick
   rice noodles (*mifen*)

Spice Paste

50 g (^{1}/$_2$ cup) chopped
   shallots
4 cm (1 ^{1}/$_2$ in) fresh turmeric
6 slices galangal
2 stalks lemongrass
1 ^{1}/$_2$ tablespoons ground
   dried red chillies
10 candlenuts (*buah keras*)
1 teaspoon shrimp paste
   (*belacan*)
1 ^{1}/$_2$ tablespoons ground
   coriander seeds
2 tablespoons dried
   shrimps, rinsed
60 ml (^{1}/$_4$ cup) water

1. To prepare Spice Paste,
grind or blend all ingredients to a smooth paste.
2. Heat oil in large
saucepan and sauté Spice
Paste until fragrant.
3. Add the stock and
bring to the boil.
4. Add coconut milk and

heat through. Do not let
the soup boil or the
coconut milk will curdle.

Chilli Oil

5 medium red chillies
1 tablespoon ground dried
   red chillies
1 teaspoon shrimp paste
   (*belacan*)
60 ml (^{1}/$_4$ cup) water
3 tablespoons oil
^{1}/$_4$ teaspoon salt
^{1}/$_4$ teaspoon sugar

1. To prepare Chilli Oil,
grind together chillies,
shrimp paste and water.
Heat oil in a small
saucepan and gently cook
ground ingredients and
the salt and sugar for
about 5 minutes until fragrant and oil rises to the
surface. The Chilli Oil
should still be fairly liquid.

 Serves 4

Preparation time:
   1 hour
Cooking time:
   30 mins

Garnish

8 quail eggs, hard-boiled
   (hard-cooked) and shelled
200 g (7 oz) prawns, boiled
   and peeled
200 g (1 ^{1}/$_2$ cups) cucumber,
   finely shredded
200 g (7 oz) chicken,
   poached and shredded
100 g (^{3}/$_4$ cup) beansprouts,
   lightly blanched
10 g (^{1}/$_2$ cup) polygonum
   leaves (*daun kesom*), finely
   chopped

1. To serve, blanche noodles in boiling water.
Drain, and place in four
serving bowls.
2. Place the garnishing
items on top of the
noodles, starting with
beansprouts, cucumber,
chicken, prawns and eggs.
3. Ladle the gravy over the
noodles. Garnish with
Chilli Oil and polygonum.
Serve immediately.

*Blend or grind the Spice Paste ingredients
until smooth.*

*Blend the small bird's-eye, or large red,
chillies with ground dried chilli for Chilli Oil.*

Daun kesom *(polygonum leaves), quail eggs and cucumber are used to garnish this dish.*

Fresh noodles need only be blanched in boiling water and drained before serving.

11

Bakwan Kepiting
(Crabmeat Ball Soup)

150 g (³/₄ cup) minced pork
200 g (1 ¹/₂ cups) shredded
  bamboo shoots
65 g (¹/₂ cup) steamed crabmeat (from about 600 g or
  1 lb 7 oz crabs, steamed)
2 teaspoons cornstarch
2 spring onions (scallions),
  finely chopped
1 ¹/₄ teaspoons salt
¹/₄ teaspoon ground white
  pepper
1 ¹/₂ litres (6 cups) chicken
  stock
5 sprigs (1 cup) chopped
  coriander (cilantro) leaves
1 tablespoons fried sliced
  shallots

 Serves 4

Preparation time:
  40 mins
Cooking time:
  10 mins

1. Mix pork with 70 g (¹/₂ cup) of the bamboo shoots, the crabmeat, cornstarch, spring onions, ¹/₂ teaspoon of the salt and some of the pepper.
2. Divide crabmeat mixture into 12 portions and roll into small balls, about 3 ¹/₂ cm (1 ¹/₂ in) in diameter.
3. Bring the stock to the boil with remaining ³/₄ teaspoon salt, 130 g (1 cup) bamboo shoots and pepper.
4. Place the balls into the boiling soup, and simmer for 5 minutes until they float to the surface.
5. Remove the soup from the heat and garnish with coriander leaves and fried shallots.

Note: If using tinned bamboo shoots, boil for 30 minutes in several changes of water before shredding to get rid of the strong smell.

Hu Piao Soup
(Fish Maw Soup)

50 g (1 ³/4 oz) fried fish maw
1 ¹/2 litres (6 cups) chicken stock
300 g (3 cups) cabbage, cut into 4 cm (1 ¹/2 in) squares
1 teaspoon salt
2 pinches ground white pepper
200 g (7 oz) abalone (optional) (about ¹/2 tin), thinly sliced
1 sprig coriander (cilantro)

Prawn Meatballs

100 g (¹/2 cup) minced pork
150 g (5 oz) blended or pounded shelled prawns
3 water chestnuts, peeled and chopped
¹/4 teaspoon salt
¹/4 teaspoon ground white pepper
1 teaspoon cornstarch

1. Soak fish maw in a large basin of cold water until soft. Remove, cut into 2 ¹/2 cm (1 in) cubes and rinse.
2. Mix Prawn Meatball ingredients together and divide into 12 portions, then roll into balls.
3. Heat stock in a large pot, add cabbage, salt, pepper and fish maw and simmer until cabbage is tender.
4. When cabbage is almost done, add Prawn Meatballs and simmer until they rise to the surface. Add any liquid from the tinned abalone and bring to the boil. Stir in sliced abalone, garnish with coriander leaves and serve hot.

Note: Although optional, abalone is a delicious addition.

 Serves 4

Preparation time:
  30 mins
Cooking time:
  30 mins

Soak the fish maw until soft then cut into cubes. Rinse clean.

Itek Tim (Duck and Salted Vegetable Soup)

 Serves 4

2 kg (4 lb 8 oz) duck
Salt to clean duck
600 g (1 lb 4 oz) salted
   mustard greens (*kiam chye*)
2 ¹/₂ litres (10 cups) water
5 cm (2 in) old ginger,
   peeled and smashed
6 preserved plums
2 tablespoons brandy
4 pieces tamarind peel
   (*asam gelugor*), rinsed
¹/₄ teaspoon ground white
   pepper
3 medium ripe tomatoes
   (about 300 g or 11 oz),
   quartered

Preparation time:
  15 mins
Cooking time:
  2 hours

Note: *This soup tastes even better if kept overnight, or for several days.*

1. Clean the duck by rubbing some salt in the cavity and on the skin. Rinse and cut the duck into four large pieces, removing any visible fat.
2. If *kiam chye* is very salty, soak for 15 minutes in several changes of water. Cut into 4 cm (1 ¹/₂ in) squares.
3. In a large stock pot, bring the water to the boil, then add the duck, ginger, plums, 1 tablespoon of the brandy, tamarind peel and pepper. Simmer gently for 1 hour, skimming the surface often to remove any fat.
4. Add *kiam chye* and simmer for a further 45 minutes, adding tomatoes 10 minutes before the end. Adjust the seasoning, if necessary. Leave the soup to stand for several hours to allow the flavours to develop. Skim the surface with paper towel to remove any remaining fat. Reheat, add remaining brandy and serve hot.

(Clockwise from top left) asam gelugor, kiam chye *and preserved plums.*

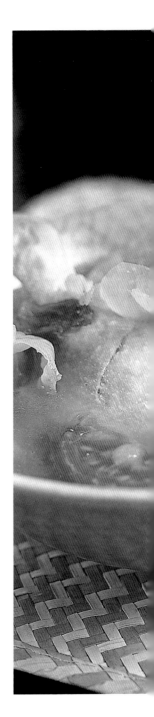

Roti Jala (Lacy Pancakes)

360 g (3 cups) plain flour
3/4 teaspoon salt
500 ml (2 cups) water
3 eggs, beaten lightly
250 ml (1 cup) thick
   coconut milk
Oil for frying

Serves 4

Preparation time:
   5 mins
Cooking time:
   20 mins

1. Sift the flour and salt into a large bowl.
2. Beat together the water, eggs and coconut milk, then whisk the mixture gently into the dry ingredients. Do not overbeat. If there are lumps, pour the batter through a sieve. Allow the batter to rest for 5 minutes.
3. Heat a flat heavy-based frying pan, Indian roti pan or non-stick crêpe pan and brush lightly with oil. The pan is hot enough when a drop of water sizzles and evaporates in a few seconds.
4. Pour 60 ml (1/4 cup) of the batter onto the pan through a roti jala cup, or any container with holes made in the base, moving it in circles to form a lacy pancake.
5. Cook for under 1 minute then fold into quarters or stack in a pile on top of each other. Cover with a towel. Repeat the process until all the mixture is used up.
6. Serve with Dry Chicken Curry with Shallots (page 34). For a sweet variation, you may like to sprinkle pancakes with icing (confectioner's) sugar and eat as a snack, as with Indian Roti Paratha.

Gently whisk the wet ingredients into the dry ingredients.

Pour the batter through a sieve to remove any lumps.

Pour the batter onto the pan through a roti jala cup or similarly shaped receptacle.

Remove the pancake gently taking care not to break it.

Asam Fish with Ladies Fingers

600 g (1 lb 5 oz) firm, white-fleshed fish (such as mackerel or threadfin)
2 tablespoons oil
2 tablespoons tamarind pulp soaked in 250 ml (1 cup) water
500 ml (2 cups) water
1 teaspoon salt
400 g (3 1/3 cups) ladies fingers (okra)

Spice Paste
100 g (1 cup) chopped shallots
1 tablespoon ground dried red chillies
4 cm (1 1/2 in) old turmeric
1/2 teaspoon shrimp paste (*belacan*)
2 stalks lemongrass
4 slices galangal
4 candlenuts (*buah keras*)
2 tablespoons water

1. Clean the fish (cut in half if using whole fish).
2. Stir and strain the tamarind water and discard pulp.
3. Blend all Spice Paste ingredients to a smooth paste then heat oil in a saucepan and sauté Spice Paste until fragrant.
4. Add tamarind water, water, salt and ladies fingers, and bring to the boil. Simmer until vegetables are firm but tender.
5. Add the fish, bring to the boil again and simmer for 5 minutes or until the fish is almost done.
6. Let the fish curry stand for several hours to allow the flavours to develop. Serve with steamed rice.

 Serves 4

Preparation time:
    20 mins
Cooking time:
    20 mins

Remove the hard tips from the ladies fingers with a sharp knife.

Stuffed Fish

600 g (1 lb 5 oz)
  whole mackerel
  (*ikan selar* or *kembong*)
1 teaspoon salt
4 tablespoons oil

 Serves 4

Preparation time:
  30 mins
Cooking time:
  10 mins

Spice Paste
25 g (¹/4 cup) chopped
  shallots
5 bird's-eye chillies
  (or 4 medium red chillies),
  deseeded
¹/2 teaspoon shrimp paste
  (*belacan*)
4 kaffir lime leaves,
  finely shredded
2 teaspoons tamarind pulp
  soaked in 2 teaspoons
  water, stirred and strained

1. To prepare whole fish for stuffing, gut the fish from the gills rather than by slitting the stomach open. Then insert a knife along the backbone, keeping the slit close to the bone to form a pocket for the stuffing. There should be two slits, one on either side of the backbone. Rub the salt into the skin of the fish.
2. To prepare the Spice Paste, blend shallots, chillies and shrimp paste until smooth. Add shredded lime leaves and tamarind water and mix well.
3. Stuff the fish with the Spice Paste mixture.
4. Heat the oil in a wok until hot, then fry the fish until golden brown on both sides. The fish is done when the eyes turn opaque.
5. Serve immediately with steamed rice.

Open the gills wide and insert a finger to gut the fish without damaging the body.

Slit pockets either side of, and close to, the backbone.

Stuff the fish with some of the Spice Paste mixture, taking care not to overstuff.

Fry the fish until golden brown on one side before turning it over to fry the other side.

Dry Sambal Fish

600 g (1 lb 5 oz) fish, such
  as mackerel (*ikan selar,*
  kembong or *tenggiri*)
1 teaspoon salt
4 tablespoons oil
60 ml (¹/4 cup) thick
  coconut milk
2 tablespoons water

Spice Paste

50 g (¹/2 cup) chopped
  shallots
3 cloves garlic
5 large fresh chillies,
  deseeded
4 cm (1 ¹/2 in) fresh turmeric
¹/2 teaspoon shrimp paste
  (*belacan*)
4 slices galangal
6 candlenuts (*buah keras*)
2 tablespoons water

1. Clean the fish and rub in ¹/2 teaspoon of the salt onto the skin of the fish. Set aside for 30 minutes.

2. To prepare the Spice Paste, blend all the ingredients to a smooth paste.

3. Heat the oil in pan and brown the fish on both sides. The fish does not need to be cooked through. Drain and set aside until required.

4. Sauté the Spice Paste in a frying pan over low heat until translucent. Add the remaining ¹/2 teaspoon salt, coconut milk, water and fried fish and simmer until the Spice Paste is thick. Insert a knife near the spine of the fish to check if it is cooked.

 Serves 4

Preparation time:
  30 mins
Cooking time:
  20 mins

Prawn Sambal with Petai

1 tablespoon tamarind pulp
  soaked in 2 tablespoons
  water
2 tablespoons oil
100 g (³/4 cup) shelled *petai*
  (also known as stink bean)
¹/2 teaspoon salt
60 ml (¹/4 cup) water
500 g (1 lb 2 oz) small
  prawns, peeled, tails intact

Spice Paste

100 g (1 cup) chopped
  shallots
2 candlenuts (*buah keras*)
1 ¹/2 tablespoons ground
  dried red chillies
2 teaspoons shrimp paste
  (*belacan*)
2 stalks lemongrass
4 slices galangal
125 ml (¹/2 cup) water

1. Stir and strain the tamarind water and discard the seeds and fibres.
2. To prepare the Spice Paste, blend all the ingredients until smooth.
3. Heat the oil in a heavy-based frying pan and sauté the Spice Paste until fragrant.
4. Add tamarind water, petai, salt and water and simmer for about 7 minutes or until the beans are almost cooked.
5. Add the prawns and cook for 2 to 3 minutes, or until the prawns turn pink.
6. Set aside for several hours to allow flavours to mature.
7. Reheat and serve with plain white rice.

 Serves 4

Preparation time:
  30 mins
Cooking time:
  15 mins

Petai beans are usually sold out of the pod.

Strain the tamarind water to remove the pulp.

Peel the prawns but leave the tails intact.

Simmer the petai before adding the prawns.

Prawns with Pineapple

400 g (14 ¹/2 oz) pineapple
  flesh (from a 600 g or
  1 lb 5 oz pineapple)
1 kg (2 lb 4 oz) medium
  prawns
1 tablespoon tamarind
  pulp softened in 125 ml
  (¹/2 cup) water
2 tablespoons oil
1 teaspoon salt
Sugar to taste (optional)

Spice Paste
100 g (1 cup) chopped
  shallots
5 medium fresh red
  chillies, deseeded
25 g (1 oz) fresh turmeric
¹/2 tablespoon shrimp
  paste (*belacan*)
2 stalks lemongrass
2 tablespoons water

1. Remove the hard core of the pineapple, then cut into wedges about 2 cm (³/4 in) thick.
2. To prepare prawns, trim off the sharp tips of the heads with scissors, leaving the head and shell intact.
3. Stir and strain the tamarind water, discarding the pulp and seeds.
4. To make the Spice Paste, blend all the ingredients until smooth.
5. Heat oil in a wok and sauté Spice Paste until fragrant.
6. Add the tamarind water, pineapple, salt and sugar, and bring to the boil. Reduce the heat, cook until pineapple becomes translucent.
7. Add the prawns and cook until they turn pink.
8. Serve with steamed rice.

Note: A ripe and very sweet pineapple would be ideal for this dish. If one is not available, use canned pineapple (but drain the syrup).

 Serves 4

Preparation time:
  20 mins
Cooking time:
  10 mins

Prawn Curry with Tomatoes

1 teaspoon tamarind pulp
  soaked in 2 teaspoons
  water
1 tablespoon oil
200 g (1 1/2 cups) ripe tomatoes, quartered
100 g (2/3 cup) onion, peeled
  and coarsely sliced
1 teaspoon salt
60 ml (1/4 cup) water
1 kg (2 lb 4 oz) large prawns,
  keep prawn whole but trim
  sharp tips of head
125 ml (1/2 cup) thick
  coconut milk

Spice Paste
100 g (1 cup) chopped
  shallots
4 cloves garlic, peeled
25 g (1 oz) fresh turmeric,
  peeled
2 stalks lemongrass
3 slices galangal
2 teaspoons shrimp paste
  (*belacan*)
25 g (1/2 cup) fresh coconut,
  grated
10 medium red chillies,
  deseeded
2 tablespoons water

1. Stir and strain the tamarind, discard any solids.
2. To prepare the Spice Paste, blend all the ingredients until smooth.
3. Heat the oil in wok and sauté the Spice Paste until soft and fragrant.
4. Add the tomatoes, onion, tamarind water, salt and 60 ml (1/4 cup) water and bring to the boil.
5. Reduce the heat and simmer for about 3 minutes until the tomatoes are soft.
6. Add the prawns and coconut milk and cook until the prawns turn pink.
7. Serve the curry with steamed rice.

 Serves 4

Preparation time:
  30 mins
Cooking time:
  20 mins

Ayam Buah Keluak (Chicken with Keluak)

30 *buah keluak* nuts to yield
   200 g (1 cup) nut meat
   (see Note below)
100 g (1 cup) minced pork
1 teaspoon salt
2 tablespoons tamarind
   pulp soaked in 250 ml
   (1 cup) water
2 tablespoons oil
1 ¹/₂ kg (3 lb 6 oz) chicken,
   quartered
1 litre (4 cups) water

Spice Paste

150 g (1 ¹/₂ cups) chopped
   shallots
4 stalks lemongrass
2 ¹/₂ cm (1 in) galangal
¹/₂ teaspoon shrimp paste
   (*belacan*)
2 tablespoons ground dried
   red chillies
125 ml (¹/₂ cup) water

 Serves 4

Preparation time:
   4 days
Cooking time:
   30 mins

To prepare buah keluak

1. Soak whole nuts in several changes of water for three days. Scrub clean.
2. Using a broad-tipped screwdriver and a pestle, knock out the little grooved plate on the nut (the traditional method of opening *buah keluak* is to use the corner of a cleaver but this is not recommended for beginners). Widen the opening further by removing some of the shell with a pair of clean, broad-tipped pliers.
3. Extract the nut meat, discarding any meat that is hard, green or smells unpleasant. The meat should be soft, black or dark brown, and fragrant.
4. Pound the nut meat until smooth.
5. Combine the minced pork, nut meat and ¹/₂ teaspoon of the salt. Stuff the mixture back into the empty *buah keluak* shells.

To prepare curry

1. Stir and strain tamarind water, discarding any solids.
2. To make Spice Paste, blend all ingredients until smooth.
3. Heat the oil in saucepan and sauté the Spice Paste until fragrant.
4. Add the chicken and sauté for 5 minutes.
5. Add the water, tamarind water, salt and stuffed *buah keluak* and bring to the boil. Reduce the heat and simmer gently for 20 minutes.
6. Leave to stand for several hours, or overnight, in the refrigerator to allow the flavours to develop (the dish may be frozen at this point and keeps well). Reheat and serve hot.

Note: Thirty keluak *nuts yield about 200 g (1 cup) nut meat provided all are perfect.*

Use a broad-tipped screwdriver and pestle to knock out the grooved plates on the nuts.

Extract the meat from the shells and discard meat that is green or unpleasant smelling.

Stuff the empty shells with the nut and meat filling.

Sauté the chicken in the Spice Paste for 5 minutes before adding the buah keluak.

33

Dry Chicken Curry with Shallots

2 tablespoons oil
4 cm (1$^1/_2$ in) cinnamon
   stick
6 cardamoms
1 kg (2 lb 4 oz) chicken, cut
   into 8 pieces
2 teaspoons sugar
125 ml ($^1/_2$ cup) thick
   coconut milk
250 ml (1 cup) water
1 teaspoon salt
2 tablespoons fried shallots

Spice Paste
2 tablespoons ground dried
   red chillies
2 tablespoons ground cumin
2 tablespoons ground fennel
1 teaspoon turmeric powder
6 cloves garlic, minced
3 tablespoons water

1. To prepare the Spice Paste, mix all the ingredients thoroughly until smooth.
2. Heat the oil in a pan and sauté the Spice Paste, the cinnamon stick and whole cardamoms until fragrant.
3. Stir in the chicken, sugar, coconut milk, water, 1 $^1/_2$ tablespoons of the fried shallots and salt and simmer gently until the chicken is cooked and the curry is almost dry. Garnish with the remaining fried shallots.
4. Serve with steamed rice, crusty French bread or Roti Jala (see page 18). If serving with Roti Jala you may prefer to double the water and Spice Paste to yield more gravy.

 Serves 4

Preparation time:
   15 mins
Cooking time:
   1 hour

Spicy Grilled Chicken

1 kg (2 lb 4 oz) chicken,
  quartered
500 ml (2 cups) thick
  coconut milk
1 teaspoon salt
2 kaffir lime leaves
2 teaspoons sugar
60 ml (1/4 cup) lime juice
250 ml (1 cup) chicken stock
  (optional)

Spice Paste
15 medium red chillies,
  deseeded
100 g (1 cup) chopped
  shallots
6 cloves garlic
4 cm (1 3/4 in) ginger
3 cm (1 3/4 in) fresh turmeric
4 slices galangal
60 ml (1/4 cup) thick
  coconut milk

Serves 4

Preparation time:
  20 mins
Cooking time:
  45 mins

1. To prepare the Spice Paste, blend all the ingredients together until smooth.

2. Transfer the Spice Paste to a large frying pan and add all the remaining ingredients except the lime juice and stock. Poach the chicken, turning frequently, for 30 minutes until the chicken is partly cooked. Remove the chicken and retain the liquid.

3. Transfer the chicken pieces to an oven-proof dish and grill or broil them under high heat for about 5 minutes on each side until browned.

4. Continue to cook the remaining poaching liquid until it reduces to a thick paste. If you prefer a more liquid gravy, you may need to add some extra coconut milk or chicken stock. Stir in the lime juice.

5. Arrange the chicken pieces on a serving dish and spoon the gravy over the meat.

6. Serve with steamed rice and pickles.

Poach the chicken in the coconut milk and Spice Paste mixture.

Grill or broil the chicken quarters until each side is browned.

Babi Pong Teh (Stewed Pork)

600 g (1 lb 5 oz) belly pork
  with skin
1 ¹/₄ tablespoons oil
100 g (1 cup) sliced shallots
1 tablespoon chopped garlic
1 tablespoon fermented soya
  beans (*dou jiang*), rinsed
  and finely mashed
200 g (7 oz) bamboo shoots,
  cut into chunks
6 cm (2 ¹/₂ in) cinnamon
1 tablespoon dark soy sauce
2 tablespoons sugar
¹/₂ teaspoon salt
¹/₄ teaspoon ground white
  pepper
1 litre (4 cups) water
4 green chillies, coarsely
  sliced

 Serves 4

Preparation time:
  30 mins
Cooking time:
  2 hours

1. To cut the belly pork into neat cubes, lay it flat on a tray and leave it in the freezer for 30 minutes to harden. Cut into 3 cm (1 ¹/₄ in) cubes.

2. Heat the oil in a saucepan and gently sauté the sliced shallots and garlic until translucent. Add the soya beans and cook for a further minute.

3. Add the pork, bamboo shoots, cinnamon, dark soy sauce, sugar, salt, pepper and water. Cover and bring to the boil, then reduce the heat and simmer for about 1 ¹/₂ hours until the meat is tender. Set aside for several hours to let the flavours develop.

4. Reheat the pork and serve with steamed rice or crusty French bread and the green chillies.

Asam Pork (Tangy Fried Pork Slices)

400 g (14 1/2 oz) pork belly,
  skin removed
2 tablespoons oil

Marinade
4 tablespoons tamarind pulp
1/2 teaspoon salt

 Serves 4

Preparation time:
  20 mins
Cooking time:
  10 mins

1. Boil the pork in a pot of water for 20 minutes. Remove and cool.
2. To prepare the Marinade, combine all the ingredients and stir well.
3. Rub the Marinade over the pork, then store overnight in a plastic bag or box in the refrigerator.
4. Before cooking, wipe the tamarind off the pork. Heat the oil in a wok and fry the pork on both sides until nicely browned.
5. Slice thinly and serve with Chilli Sauce.

Note: Makes a great snack to accompany drinks.

Garlic Chilli Sauce

5 medium red chillies,
  deseeded
2 cloves garlic
1 tablespoon rice vinegar
1/4 tablespoon salt
1 teaspoon sugar

1. Blend together until fine. Good with deep-fried foods such as spring rolls, and fried meats like chicken.

Pork Sambal

2 tablespoons oil
600 g (1 lb 5 oz) lean pork,
   sliced thinly into 3 cm
   (1 1/4 in) strips
1/2 teaspoon sugar
1 teaspoon salt
125 ml (1/2 cup) water
60 ml (1/4 cup) thick
   coconut milk

Spice Paste
2 pieces 4 cm (1 1/2 in)
   fresh turmeric, peeled
10 medium red chillies,
   deseeded
4 slices galangal
2 tablespoons water

1. To prepare the Spice Paste, blend all the ingredients until smooth.
2. Heat the oil in a wok and gently cook the Spice Paste for about 5 minutes until the oil rises to the surface and the paste becomes fragrant.
3. Add the pork, sugar, salt, water and coconut milk. Bring to the boil, then simmer gently until the oil rises to the surface once more.
4. Serve with plain rice.

 Serves 4

Preparation time:
   15 mins
Cooking time:
   15 mins

41

Braised Pig's Trotters in Sweet-Sour Sauce

400 g (14 1/2 oz) fresh
  pineapple, peeled
2 tablespoons oil
1 1/2 kg (3 lb 6 oz) pig's
  trotters, cut into 5 cm
  (2 in) pieces
1/2 teaspoon dark soy sauce
4 tablespoons tamarind
  pulp soaked in 250 ml
  (1 cup) water, stirred and
  strained
1/2 teaspoon salt
2 teaspoons sugar
1 litre (4 cups) water

Spice Paste
100 g (1 cup) chopped
  shallots
10 cloves garlic, chopped
2 tablespoons ground
  dried red chillies
60 ml (1/4 cup) water

 Serves 4

Preparation time:
  30 mins
Cooking time:
  2 1/2 hours

1. Peel and quarter the pineapple, removing the hard centre. Cut into slices 1 cm (1/2 in) thick.
2. To make the Spice Paste, blend all the ingredients to a smooth paste.
3. Heat the oil in a large saucepan and sauté the Spice Paste until fragrant.
4. Add the pork, dark soy sauce, tamarind water, salt, sugar and water. Bring to the boil, then reduce the heat and simmer for about 1 1/2 hours until the meat is tender but still has a firm texture.
5. Add the pineapple slices and gently cook for a further 3 minutes or until the pineapple is soft and translucent. Remove from the heat.
6. Leave to stand for several hours to allow the flavours to develop.
7. Reheat and serve with steamed rice.

Babi Chin (Fragrant Pork)

600 g (1 lb 5 oz) cubed pork belly or 1 kg (2 lb 4 oz) boneless pork leg, chopped into chunks
3 tablespoons oil
100 g (1 cup) sliced shallots
6 cloves garlic, sliced
1 tablespoon ground coriander seeds
4 star anise
8 large dried shiitake mushrooms, softened in water
1 tablespoon dark soy sauce

1 teaspoon sugar
1/2 teaspoon salt
1/4 teaspoon ground white pepper
1 litre (4 cups) water

 Serves 4

Preparation time:
   30 mins
Cooking time:
   2 hours

1. To cut pork belly into neat cubes, lay it flat on a large plate and leave it in the freezer for 30 minutes to harden. Remove and cut into 3 cm (1 1/4 in) cubes. If using pork leg, rinse the meat well (ask the butcher to chop it into chunks).
2. Heat oil in a large saucepan and brown the shallots and garlic until fragrant. Add coriander and star anise, and cook for 1 minute.
3. Squeeze any excess water from the mushrooms and add to the pan with the pork, soy sauce, sugar, salt, pepper and water. Bring to the boil, then reduce the heat and simmer for about 1 1/2 to 2 hours until the meat is tender.
4. Set the dish aside for several hours at room temperature to allow the flavours to develop.
5. Reheat and serve with plain rice or crusty French bread. Garnish with diced red chilli if desired.

Slicing pork is made easier if the meat is frozen briefly beforehand.

Beef Rendang

1 kg (2 lb 4 oz) lean beef
  (blade, chuck, round or
  skirt steak) cut into 3 cm
  (1 1/4 in) cubes
1 teaspoon salt
4 cm (1 3/4 in) galangal,
  peeled and smashed
2 stalks lemongrass, peeled
  and smashed
2 teaspoons sugar
1/2 tablespoon tamarind
  soaked in 125 ml (1/2 cup)
  water, stirred and strained
250 ml (1 cup) thick coconut
  milk
375 ml (1 1/2 cups) water

Spice Paste
50 g (1/2 cup) chopped
  shallots
25 g (1/2 cup) toasted
  coconut
2 slices old ginger
1 tablespoon ground dried
  red chillies
2 tablespoons ground
  coriander seeds
1/2 tablespoon ground fennel
125 ml (1/2 cup) water

Serves 4

Preparation time:
  15 mins
Cooking time:
  1 1/2 hours

1. To make the Spice Paste, blend or grind all the
ingredients until smooth.
2. In a saucepan, combine the Spice Paste with all other
ingredients and bring to the boil.
3. Reduce the heat and simmer gently for 1 1/2 hours or
until the beef is tender. Add extra liquid if required.
4. Serve with plain rice or bread.

*Toast grated coconut before adding it to the
Spice Paste.*

Cut beef into bite-sized cubes.

Chap Chye (Mixed Vegetables Stew)

4 large dried shiitake mushrooms, soaked in 125 ml ($^{1}/_{2}$ cup) warm water

4 tablespoons oil

1 tablespoon chopped garlic

1 tablespoon fermented soya beans (*dou jiang*), mashed

2 litres (8 cups) Pork Stock (see recipe below)

1 teaspoon salt

30 g (1 oz) beansticks, softened and cut into finger lengths

100 g (3 $^{3}/_{4}$ oz) yam bean (jicama), cut into 5 cm x 5 mm (2 in x $^{1}/_{4}$ in) batons

7 g ($^{1}/_{2}$ oz) woodears, softened in water and trimmed

15 g ($^{1}/_{4}$ cup) golden lily buds, knotted and soaked in 1 tablespoon water

30 g (1 oz) glass noodles, softened in 250 ml (2 cups) water

100 g (1 cup) cabbage, cut into 4 cm (1 $^{1}/_{2}$ in) squares

3 red dates (optional)

10 g ($^{1}/_{3}$ oz) sweet beancurd, softened in water, quartered

100 g (3 $^{1}/_{2}$ oz) small prawns, sharp tips removed from heads

1. Remove the hard stem from the mushrooms and reserve the water.

2. Heat the oil in large stockpot and sauté the garlic until fragrant. Add the soya beans and cook for 1 minute, then add the Pork Stock, mushroom water and salt and bring to the boil.

3. Add the beansticks, yam bean, shiitake mushrooms, wood ears, lily buds, glass noodles, cabbage and red dates (optional) and simmer gently for about 15 minutes or until the yam bean is soft.

4. Add the beancurd and prawns and bring to the boil. Remove from the heat.

5. Serve with Sambal Belacan and rice, if desired.

Note: This post-Lunar New Year dish uses the dried ingredients traditionally used as offerings to the gods. The soup tastes better when kept overnight. Take care to boil again and cool before storing in the fridge.

 Serves 4

Preparation time:
  2 hours
Cooking time:
  30 mins

Pork Stock

1.5 kg (3 lb 6 oz) pork ribs

2.5 litres (10 cups) water

A few white peppercorns

Combine all ingredients in a large pot and simmer for at least 2 hours to yield about 2 litres (8 cups) Pork Stock.

Spicy Pork and Vegetable Stew

50 g (2 1/2 cups) tamarind pulp soaked in 125 ml (1/2 cup) water
1 kg (2 lb 4 oz) bitter mustard greens
1 1/2 kg (3 lb 6 oz) roasted chicken bones or pork spare ribs (see Note)
4 litres (16 cups) water
3 stalks lemongrass, smashed
2 tablespoons ground dried red chilli
20 g (1/2 cup) tamarind peel (*asam gelugor*)
1 teaspoon salt
1 teaspoon shrimp paste (*belacan*)

 Serves 4

Preparation time:
10 mins
Cooking time:
3 hours

1. Strain tamarind water, discard seeds and fibres.
2. Rinse the mustard greens and cut into 4 cm (1 1/2 in) squares.
3. Combine all the ingredients in a large stock pot and bring to the boil. Simmer gently for three hours until the vegetables are soft and the liquid has reduced by three-quarters.
4. Serve with steamed rice.

Note: This is a perfect stew to prepare after the Lunar New Year period as it is a good way to use up leftover roasts, ribs, fried chicken or pork, and makes a delicious contrast to the rich festive dishes.

Cucumber Kerabu with Pork
(Spicy Pork and Cucumber Salad)

200 g (7 oz) pork belly, skin
  removed
250 g (9 oz) cucumber
25 g (¼ cup) thinly sliced
  shallots
30 g (¼ cup) dried shrimps,
  soaked and ground
1 tablespoon Sambal Belacan
1 tablespoon lime juice
½ teaspoon salt
Sugar to taste
3 sprigs (½ cup) chopped
  coriander (cilantro) leaves

1. Place pork belly in a saucepan of boiling water. When water returns to the boil, lower heat and simmer for about 18 minutes until cooked. Cool, then slice thinly.
2. Peel cucumber, discard top and bottom, then quarter it lengthways and discard the soft centre. Slice thinly.
3. Mix sliced shallots with dried prawns, Sambal Belacan, lime juice, salt and sugar. Add cucumber, pork and coriander and mix well.
4. Serve with rice.

 Serves 4

Preparation time:
  20 mins
Cooking time:
  15 mins

Terung Lemak
(Aubergines in Coconut Gravy)

600 g (1 lb 6 oz)
  aubergine (eggplant)
2 tablespoons oil
250 ml (1 cup) thick
  coconut milk
250 ml (1 cup) water
1/2 teaspoon salt

Spice Paste
50 g (1/2 cup) chopped
  shallots
2 tablespoons dried
  shrimps
5 medium fresh red
  chillies, deseeded
1/2 teaspoon shrimp paste
  (*belacan*)

1. Slice aubergine about 1 cm (1/2 in) thick.
2. Lightly brush slices with oil and dry-fry in a pan over low heat; alternatively grill or bake in a moderate oven for 10 minutes. The aubergine does not need to be cooked through.
3. To prepare the Spice Paste, blend all the ingredients to a smooth paste.
4. Sauté Spice Paste in 1 tablespoon oil until fragrant.
5. Add the water, coconut cream, salt and aubergine and simmer until the vegetable is soft.
6. Serve with steamed rice.

 Serves 4

Preparation time:
  20 mins
Cooking time:
  35 mins

Sweet Potato and Kai Lan Lemak
(Vegetables in Coconut Gravy)

300 g (11 oz) sweet potato
Juice of 1 lemon
600 g (1 lb 5 oz) *kai lan*
  (kale), or baby *kai lan*
1 tablespoon oil
125 ml (1/2 cup) thick
  coconut milk
500 ml (2 cups) water
1/2 teaspoon salt

Spice Paste
50 g (1/2 cup) chopped
  shallots
2 tablespoons dried shrimps,
  cleaned
5 fresh red chillies, deseeded
1/2 teaspoon shrimp paste
  (*belacan*)
2 tablespoons water

1. Peel the sweet potato and cut into 2 1/2 cm (1 in) chunks. Set aside in a bowl of water with lemon juice to prevent it from turning black.
2. Cut the *kai lan* into finger lengths.
3. To prepare the Spice Paste, blend all the ingredients to a smooth paste.
4. Heat the oil in a saucepan and toast the Spice Paste until fragrant.
5. Add the sweet potato, water and coconut milk. Simmer until almost soft.
6. Add the *kai lan* and cook for a further 1 to 2 minutes.
7. Serve with steamed rice.

 Serves 4

Preparation time:
  15 mins
Cooking time:
  15 mins

Pound or blend all the Spice Paste ingredients until smooth.

Ladies Fingers in Sambal Belacan

500 g (4 cups) ladies fingers
  (okra), small, fresh and
  crisp
2 tablespoons oil
2 cloves garlic, minced
1 teaspoon Sambal Belacan
100 g (1 cup) small prawns,
  peeled
1 teaspoon tamarind pulp in
  1 tablespoon water
250 ml (1 cup) water
1/2 teaspoon salt

 Serves 4

Preparation time:
  10 mins
Cooking time:
  10 mins

1. Remove the dark tips and tops from the ladies fingers (okra).
2. Heat the oil in a wok, then sauté the garlic and Sambal Belacan until fragrant.
3. Add the prawns, ladies fingers, water, tamarind water and salt, and simmer until the ladies fingers are tender but still firm.
4. Serve hot with steamed rice.

Note: Other vegetables which may be used in this dish in place of ladies fingers are long beans and French beans.

Sambal Kangkung (Stir-fried Spicy Greens)

1 kg (5 cups) water convolvulus (*kangkung*)
1 tablespoon oil
1/4 teaspoon salt
1 tablespoon water
1 teaspoon tamarind pulp soaked in 1 tablespoon water, stirred and strained
2 teaspoons light soy sauce

Spice Paste

25 g (1/4 cup) chopped shallots
1 clove garlic
1 tablespoon fermented soya beans (*dou jiang*)
1/2 teaspoon shrimp paste (*belacan*)
3 medium red chillies, deseeded
2 tablespoons water

1. Wash the *kangkung* and cut into 5 cm (2 in) lengths, keeping the leaf and stem intact. Split any thick stems in half.
2. Blend all the Spice Paste ingredients until smooth then heat oil in wok and sauté Spice Paste until fragrant.
3. Add *kangkung*, salt, water, tamarind water and soy sauce and toss for 2 minutes until leaves become limp. Do not overcook.

Note: *To keep the vitamin C in green vegetables, always clean them before cutting, not afterwards. Cut vegetables just prior to cooking to preserve vitamin content longer.*

 Serves 4

Preparation time:
    20 mins
Cooking time:
    5 mins

Pengat
(Yam and Bananas in Sweet Coconut Milk)

200 g (³/4 cup) sweet potato
200 g (³/4 cup) yam
4 ripe large bananas (*pisang rajah*) (about 500 g or 1 lb 2 oz), sliced 1 cm (¹/2 in) thick and steamed until soft
1 litre (4 cups) water
125 ml (¹/2 cup) thick coconut milk
6 screwpine (*pandan*) leaves, rinsed and knotted together
250 ml (1 cup) Palm Sugar Syrup
2 large pinches salt

1. Peel the sweet potato and yam and cut into 1 cm (¹/2 in) cubes. Peel the bananas and cut into 1 cm (¹/2 in) slices. Steam the sweet potato, yam and bananas until soft.
2. Place the sweet potatoes, yam and bananas into a saucepan containing water, coconut milk, screwpine leaves, Palm Sugar Syrup and salt and bring to the boil.
3. Serve hot in individual bowls.

 Serves 4

Preparation time:
   20 mins
Cooking time:
   10 mins

Palm Sugar Syrup

400 g (1 ³/4 cup) palm sugar
250 ml (1 cup) water

 *Makes 1 ³/4 cups*

Preparation time:
   5 mins
Cooking time:
   5 mins

1. Melt the palm sugar in water in a small saucepan over low heat.
2. Cool the syrup, strain, then pour into sterilised jars.
3. Store in the refrigerator until required.

Melt the palm sugar in water in a saucepan over low heat.

After cooling and straining the syrup, pour into sterilised jars.

Bubor Terigu (Coconut Milk Porridge)

110 g (1/2 cup) wheat kernels (*terigu*)
4 screwpine (*pandan*) leaves, rinsed and knotted together
1 litre (4 cups) water
Pinch of salt
4 tablespoons Palm Sugar Syrup (see page 58)
60 ml (1/4 cup) thick coconut milk

 Serves 4

Preparation time:
    10 mins
Cooking time:
    2 hours

1. Remove any stones or foreign matter from the *terigu* and wash well.
2. Place the *terigu*, screwpine leaves and the water in a saucepan and simmer for about two hours, stirring occasionally to prevent sticking. The *terigu* should be soft but still slightly chewy.
3. Add salt and Palm Sugar Syrup and return to the boil.
4. Add the coconut milk and stir well until hot, but do not boil. Remove the screwpine leaves.
5. Serve hot.

Kuih Bingka Ubi Kayu (Tapioca Cake)

Large piece banana leaf, wiped clean
1 kg (2 lb 4 oz) peeled tapioca
190 ml (³/4 cup) water
125 ml (¹/2 cup) thick coconut milk
250 ml (1 cup) Palm Sugar Syrup

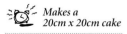 *Makes a
20cm x 20cm cake*

Preparation time:
  30 mins
Baking time:
  1 hour 10 mins

1. Preheat oven to 180°C (350°F, gas mark 4).
2. Soften banana leaf by plunging it into boiling water for 20 seconds. Remove and set aside
3. In a food processor, blend the tapioca with water until smooth.
4. Stir in the coconut milk and Palm Sugar Syrup.
5. Line a cake tin with banana leaf, making diagonal slits in the corners to enable a good fit. Pour in the batter.
6. Bake for 1 hour 10 minutes. Cool in the tin.
7. Cut into 2 cm x 5 cm (³/4 in x 2 in) slices.

Kuih Koci (Coconut–Rice Pyramids)

15 banana leaf circles
  (35 cm or 14 in) diameter
375 ml (1 1/2 cups) water
12 screwpine (*pandan*)
  leaves, washed
300 g (3 cups) glutinous rice
  flour
Pinch salt
2–3 drops green food
  colouring (optional)
1 tablespoon oil

 Makes 12

Preparation time:
  45 mins
Cooking time:
  30 mins

1. Soften banana leaves in boiling water before cutting them with kitchen scissors into 35 cm (14 in) diameter circles. Pat leaves dry with kitchen towel.
2. Make the Coconut Filling and set side until required.
3. In a food processor, blend the *pandan* leaves with the water. Strain, discarding pulp.
4. Mix the *pandan* water with rice flour to form a soft dough. If desired, add some green food colouring.
5. Lightly brush one side of a banana leaf with oil. Form it into a cone and place 60 ml (1/4 cup) batter into the cone. Press in a ball of Coconut Filling, then cover with 1 tablespoon of dough. Fold the edges over to form a pyramid and place it, flat side facing down onto a steamer. Repeat the process to make remaining cakes.
6. Steam the cakes for 15 minutes and serve.

Coconut Filling

150 g (1 1/2 cups) grated
  coconut
75 g (1/3 cup) palm sugar
4 tablespoons water

 *Makes 12 balls*

Preparation time:
  10 mins
Cooking time:
  5 mins

1. Melt palm sugar in water. Remove any foreign matter.
2. Add coconut and cook for 5 minutes, stirring constantly.
3. When the mixture is completely cool, divide the filling into 12 portions and roll each one into a ball.

Cut the banana leaves into circles.

Strain blended screwpine leaves, discard pulp.

Fold each banana leaf circle into a cone.

Stuff cones with batter and a coconut ball.

Index